T0338866

THE GINSENG HUNTER'S NOTEBOOK

The New Issues Press Poetry Series

Editor	Herbert Scott
Associate Editor	David Dodd Lee
Advisory Editors	Nancy Eimers, Mark Halliday William Olsen, J. Allyn Rosser
Assistant to the Editor	Rebecca Beech
Assistant Editors	Scott Bade, Allegra Blake, Becky Cooper, Jeff Greer, Gabrielle Halko, Matthew Hollrah, Nancy Hall James, Alexander Long, Tony Spicer, Bonnie Wozniak
Editorial Assistants	Kevin Oberlin, Matthew Plavnick, Diana Valdez
Business Manager	Michele McLaughlin
Fiscal Officer	Marilyn Rowe

The New Issues Press Poetry Series is sponsored by The College of Arts and
Sciences, Western Michigan University, Kalamazoo, Michigan

The publication of this book is made possible by a grant from
the National Endowment for the Arts.

An Inland Seas Poetry Book

 Inland Seas poetry books are supported by a grant from
The Michigan Council for Arts and Cultural Affairs.

First Edition, 1999.

ISBN: 0-932826-71-7 (cloth)
ISBN: 0-932826-72-5 (paper)

Library of Congress Cataloging-in-Publication Data:
Lundin, Deanne
The Ginseng Hunter's Notebook / Deanne Lundin
Library of Congress Catalog Card Number (98-67449)

Art Direction:	Tricia Hennessy
Design and Photography:	Jef Lear
Production:	Paul Sizer The Design Center, Department of Art College of Fine Arts Western Michigan University
Printing:	Courier Corporation
Illustration of orbits:	From *Mathematical Astronomy for Amateurs* by E.A. Beet. Copyright © 1972. Reprinted by permission of W.W. Norton & Company, Inc.

^{THE} **GINSENG HUNTER'S NOTEBOOK**

DEANNE LUNDIN

New Issues Press

WESTERN MICHIGAN UNIVERSITY

For all my families and especially for Doris

Contents

Acknowledgements

The Georgia Review: "Shaker Dance"

Prairie Schooner: "Camellias for P," "Fig," "Gladiolus,"
    "Surinam," "Four Thieves Vinegar," "Where the Soul Is"

Third Coast: "The Ginseng Hunter Finds Jimsonweed,"
    "The Ginseng Hunter Explains," "The Ginseng Hunter
    Lies Down in a Meadow"

Shenandoah: "1001 Nights"

Kenyon Review: "Poppies," "Chicory Seeds"

Colorado Review: "Lycos Search"

Antioch Review: "In This Direction"

Thus when anyone comes to a city which is strange to him, he should thoroughly examine its situation, how it lies with respect to the winds and to the sun's rising; for a city exposed to the north has not the same qualities as one exposed to the south, nor one lying towards the rising sun the same as one turned towards its setting.

Hippocrates

I

Shaker Dance

The visitor pushes the gate and it disappears

into a blue shade through which
dazzle slants in sharp white
lines like envy.

He arrives in his black box
looking for exits.

So much space
offends him.

Here we tilt away from the world

in a different gravity
where motion does not
complete.

So far we do not lie down
but square our bodies
to the ultimate task.

We keep the soul
from flying off on its string of light

though the strain pulls us up
a little each day.

Gesture becomes us.

A knot of fire undoes the hand
and it opens. The shears dip
and flash, and a green smell rises

into the rolled-up morning's
oblique news.

In a little while
the body will unfold
in all its senseless and extravagant delight,

which to the visitor will seem
like silence,

silence and arrested motion.

We call this grace.

The Ginseng Hunter Explains

To what I can't hear I am always listening,

hard as it gets each day
to remember convergence, this leaning

of foxglove over the sage
like a silent alarm: *where is the oak?*

Where is the oak?

Rainwater curls in the hole.
No note from the landlord, "sorry—the city,"

etcetera, "hazard"
and "fine,"—all the usual reasons we give

for not wanting the trouble
of life,

and so on and still endlessly on wheels disaster,
seeding little deaths like money.

Here's where my elbow squares to the door,

every hair points
to the shadow unlocking its suitcase.

Who am I kidding? Really the only
terror we face is the truth about God (Who is Love),

and we know what that means, but we'll never
be able to say it.

Now where the oak spread
its gospel of green between neighbors

there are houses standing apart
without touching: rise, o ghost,

from my door

to that roof in an arc of electric blue,
for I fear

She's forgotten me, root branch and twig.

Saturday 3PM

Bottlebrush bushes explode in a clean impatience,
red bristles soft to the touch. The day's blue
has withdrawn with its glass of iced tea
somewhere beyond the ocean's repeated

gesture of arrival, zipping, unzipping the coast,
which has nothing in common with the cypress
whose pointed hair proves we are still
falling. What connections there are may be blurred,

I admit, never having been sure how the mind
holds a vanishing point in focus
while bleached oak trees waver in a stunned remoteness
of light. We can't go on like this,

discussion is futile, I say, dialing your number,
and *When can I see you again?* throaty
as a cat in heat, leaving my own peculiar
scent among the bouquet of voices

on your scratched, well-used machine.

The Ginseng Hunter Thinks About Oranges in May

A frond does splits
like the eighth-grade cheerleader
whose mother killed off
the competition's mom
with true corporate reasoning,
able to bear looking at horror without blinking
once she accepted the heat
but this

was in Texas, some little town where dear god
hatred is frequently colorless.
Bitter almond

and oranges say all there is to be known
about light, how it struggles
out of its cave where the rock has fallen,
rounding the curve of rock
pocked like an orange. Echo
of red sky. My Florida

never was like this.
Oh we
had our casual killings,
the woman found strangled
on her round satin bed. Anyone
could have told her
what to expect from white satin,
but nobody did. Oranges
remained oranges, and so she died,
fooled by the early light
licking his face like a cat,
missing the truth of his climax,
those hard green elderberry eyes

even the birds won't light on. This
opacity of oranges

surprises a number of people each year
who come to preserve in snapshots
the effects of light shocking water,
and to eat palm dates rolled in coconut
imported like refugees
swimming up from the islands
or down from New York.
Naranja is something my father will never say,
turning his back on Miami and *platanos*,
tending his little grove of oranges.

The Ginseng Hunter Thinks About Oranges in October

Cats are like clocks.
In the window, they tick and whirr to keep traffic moving,
winding the cars in counterpoint

over the sunslicks
and into the candied crunch of leaves.

New air unwraps each appointment successively bitter
or tart. Everything hurries to get. Even my hands

smell like pennies. We know that disasters
are timed events when we hear so much brilliance harden and
    swerve
the instant we pull down the shade.

Clouds take us in like manna.
Clouds spit us out.

Winter approaches Lake Tyner, ashamed to be seen in Orlando
as the bloodoranges mass in the grove like malignancies
and memories swell like Billy McPherson
who swims, a drowned face in my dreams, because once
he believed I was wearing a bra and I kept my shirt on,
which is all I regret.

Each day repairs itself, hurricanes pass,
and the neighbors install a new generator.
All they ask is a really deep freeze.

Each night the envelopes steam themselves open.

Each night I rise through the ceiling like rain in ascension
and still have not broken the bottle.

Voulez-vous coucher avec moi was the frenchiest song we knew,
teaching our bodies tricks with the metronome
so that soon we could rinse our teeth clean
in faultless rhythm, timing the sky's
rehearsals of bliss.

Where the Soul Is

Descartes kept his in the pineal gland, safe and convenient. Even when traveling. He always knew where he was. Freud wasn't sure but felt something unusual in the penis, and thought at once of wanderers haunting the steppes, women keening the soul that flew out of them, so many exits you could not guard them all. Some keep their souls in clay jars, the scent of ground cumin and cinnamon spitting in oil, or like Yeats, in a smell of invisible violets. It lurks in a tub of laundry, in Emerson's eye. Socrates thought it had something to do with dryness, thinking perhaps of Lethe, or maybe the weight of light, his soul never happy, twisting itself in a question, kicking its legs. They say Baudelaire kept his in a bottle of wine, Picasso hacked and slashed and tore to let it out. And Beethoven's lived in his ear, just think of those terrible years of separation—or was it enclosure? private garden? festive little parties for two as he roared singing through the fields? A farmer heard him coming, stunned for a moment, was this the devil at last, coming to claim—and quickly dropped his soul, seed by seed, into its rich black holes, just in case. The divine Miss D kept hers in a tiny box. Like Beethoven, there were two of them. Tea and a crumb of blood. But she had that window, a woman's soul can always get out. I used to think my soul was gnomish, home in its hollow stump under the bridge, its sign at the crossroads. Then for a time the killing pace of her long legs covering tundra, hungry and sharp. But last night I heard her tiny hooves clatter in a panic of glee down the dividing street, dim far shriek of tea. If you love something, it's time, say the clocks, and empty, say the baskets, the lamp says, too hot, but I never let her go. She leaves when she wants to, lives where she can. She never tells me anything.

Weathering St. Cloud

Sky breaking for cover
     and finding nowhere to go cherishes clouds
that press us into the mud.
Twisted flowers
       of spine and mirth.

And then rain   like taking our clothes off after church.

So much of you seems to be there
     and then suddenly drifts.
                       Stigmata
of shudder and shrug
       while hugging the one truth tight.

The fragrance of lakewater
purges you even of that.

You open a beer.

East Lake Tohopekaliga stains each minute precisely,
blue herons and anhingas like feathered
extensions of cypress.

You don't think of its name
as an infinite hunger   cries
                  long flown
in the cry of the birds still echoing
  —ho
      to—
       ho,
  to—
    ho

like a southern mocking of expensive snow.

I keep asking to see the ocean.

        I am sure we should not be here where our voices
flit like mosquitoes. Our johnboat threatens to swamp

and I'm bailing away
   while you light up a Malboro   smiling.

It's called scoliosis. Here, I say, look it up: your back
                          twists into a question

but you don't trust words, their tricky migrations. They wait at
the airport like gifts from Finland. Letters submerged and rising:
your painful pause before spelling tire—

               "t -i -e -r"

            and the bark of astonished laughter that wilts
            you into your chair like a day-old hyacinth
            dried on an oar.

Beneath us reeds rub like paper ripped from a gift and I've nothing
to say but thanks. Gratitude's not what I feel

                    seeps into every corner I've lived in
                       awash with the weedy greens
                            of its shallow deeps

I make an effort: *Don't let disaster*
fool you into thinking

                    something better has got to be on the way.

And *Get out*

         while you still can.

        The transfusion begins. My veins open slowly, like lilies.

"Shut up," you hiss and point: swirl of green water.

        Mallards rise with the sound of old carpets
               and the huge gnarled head
sinks back, disappointed.

                  And then

                        clouds

II

In the Roof Garden

> Starved blossoms stage a comeback. Drift of
> langostina climbs the stairs.
> I forget burnt mornings, caffeine-starched and
> plumed, vociferous days.
> I want to be calm about this. I want to be fair.
> I name each pot a remedy: *Plausible, Blemish, Catch, In Sight.*
>
> Rosemary flares its tiny stash of blue as if
> blue were an easy thing anyone could do.
>
> Jewel of disasters, my sweet calamity, you are futures trading
> themselves for a past unlocking its luggage and scattering
> all of it in the street, a clamor of yellow and white,
> traffic pumping its flammable blood
> at the light, a fury and stench of sadness dressed
> in joy, and without you I have no peace.

Herbal Remedies

Juniper

Five o'clock's falling light, crushed from juniper
berries, held in little pockets of ice
the way windows harden against rain,

though the smell of rain keeps falling through
like a voice not heard, but remembered.
Such a slight tree, the juniper, twisted, sparse,

to have become a window, a view of ice
in all its meltings and freezings, rain, ice,
rain—the tongue's window falling on bitter times.

Hard luck, when juniper's light is the light you read by,
seeing in ice juniper's thirst for rain,
while desire falls in at the darkened window,

the window you surely closed. A light
matter. But the smell of *him* falling into every corner:
an icy smell of juniper, laced with rain.

Wild Onions

We think things are fine, little plates on the gold-flecked formica
under control. The sky doles out its visions to the few and the pure,
mostly in New Mexico, while massing its greater effects of fog
for the ones who will need it. Rhapsodies at the sink! Listen:
National Geographic can take us to places they've never been
with only one white man, a camera, and a couple of guides, on
the *Search for the Great Apes* which however long it takes
we know we will find.
           And there they are! silverbacked male
gorillas sitting in brine-soaked weeds, munching on shrimp
and wild onions, and aren't you surprised? They'd like us to be
a little surprised about this. How I should like to run my fingers
through your silverfine, savage hair, dripping with onions.

Eyebright

Elsewhere, the days remove layers of doubt
The way new stars confirm our suspicion
That birth is what happens when we are out
Looking for answers. Light from the Pleistocene

Era illumines your eye in its tight fit
At the telescope. Briny little puffs
Of air from the shore leave your mouth
As stray marks of guiltless violence,

Air bleeding smoke into darkness,
Keeping you pure. It's the way bitterness

Cures. Exfoliation. Purge. Blank.
And we become Us, quick as a wink.
Sofabed. One cat. Double sink.

Ginger Snaps

For the will is like a fire, baking each deed as if in a furnace.
Hildegard of Bingen

Fire's easy to mistake, its direction, its speed,
although earthquakes are also confusing. Into the oven
with you, my dear, and the toasty bits will feed
dozens for days. Little hot cross buns.
Olives! Raisins! Vienna sausage, what fun.
Gingerbread studded with everything.
Savor the sharp sweets striking the tongue, sing,
sing like cats in the furnace. Now scream. Rattle
your bones when you dance with me, dance with me,
don't be so coy. They ship the stuff in a tattered
gunny sack, roots like the members a witch gathered
into a tree-nest, as gravely recorded in *Malleus
Malificarum*. Really, come on, snap into it. Dance like it matters.

Garlic Blossom

Gold beats the air with dull rage. Who really gives a fig?
All of my mouth with an   ache. You're the way karma
rolls up its scarf while it's   raining so the punctured scar
lies perfectly hidden   like lives invisibly ill
in plain view. Convince me   it's not fatal. Beautifully
cold cash. Love in a fis   cal swoon on its back

blissfully counting its   blessings which suddenly throb
like your voice in my tune   less ear, in the dried small
offerings of sweet words   out of all passion. And how
sad it all is, anti   septic and pure at the cross-
shunted roads of our days.   Surely we should have smelled its
odious perfume, sending   out flare after flare now:
more sorrow, more hope and   more riddles of guilt to come.

Sowing Basil

(semer le basilic, "to sow basil": to rave)

Semer le basilic the French say faced with
                    farming another fistful of
basil, raving in parallel rows. *Sacrebleu*
                    basil to blooming hell and back—

hell, you can hear the hissing of
                    hard times about to hit hurricane
watch. What you want, what I want
                    wait in the waves' white warnings.

We line up like licorice, links to the
                    lasting sweetness of leathery joys.
Bad seeds, reluctant to sprout. De-
                    spite swamis who whisper blessings

and preachers who pray for peace,
                    our perfection's delayed. We're impervious.
Worse, we don't worry. War's
                    for the weak who can't wreak their own

havoc at home. Honey, I've cleaned the
                    house, I say, holding the poker handy
while you call the cops to come
                    cart me away. Too late. I'm contagious.

Springtime in Provence, the people
                        push seedlings in place. They privately
curse the dank clouds, the chill
                        clods that stick to cold fingers

and everything else about us
                        I've invented. A woman in Ireland said once
No fuck, no fight; no fight, no fuck.
                        Parallel pals in the fast track.

Fennel

Gleams in its porcelain. Handfuls. Fistfuls. Pockets
Of sweet seed. Blown like the petals of white

Bougainvillea, seeding the street with its possible
Futures, threading the air that it not detach

From its cities where color is hoarded and sold.
Waiters, in cinnamon glimpses, are bearing me

Dishes of scent I can no longer hold. O sweet
Persian boy, I am stealing your fennel from

Under the register, secretly, charmingly,
Taking it all, there's no hurry, O let the air

Scatter and turn, let the world sweeten
Its teeth for the nightly encounters, flesh in its yielding

Surprises, flesh in its sky-ground hues, and the sky
With its open-mouthed kisses of fennel.

The King Majesty's Excellent Recipe for the Plague

(nutmeg, treacle, and angelica water beaten together)

May 8. Feast of St. Michael the Archangel.

All day the angels cross and recross the street. Only I can see them. One of them offers me nutmeg, the other a toffee. We bow politely. I offer my sleepless nights, and the words of a song I don't understand, something heard once in Latvia from a street-vendor hawking angelica. He didn't know what the words meant, either. Angel Two puts a necklace over my head, made of leaves. I feel the swamps of Florida calling me out on a mission for I shall separate water hemlock from *angelica atropurpurea*, gliding above the stench of things mixing together. All day dark green has infused my vision, the roar of the T dims the street. *You can eat this*, Angel One is saying, or else, *You can beat this*, or possibly, *Two can meet: kiss*. Like the song I don't know. He puts a crown on the head of a boy with his boom box cranked to the max. The bruise slowly widens, the heart slows. It was 1665 and the plague was raging. So was the King. It must be stopped. It is intolerable. Not only what, but how things are mixed, said the witches, and then the physicians, who thought of angelica root like the angels, descending, not as we'd hoped, to heal, but to trouble the waters, descending because we were beaten enough to ask.

Poppies

hum in electric reds: light
hearted

means we see that way
       through
              music
distant
and too close to hear
          without

poppies

listen as the day shuts down
       and all things tilt toward
            difference

(which is not distinction)

poppies

sway a little
         this way
      and that

they know how much we want to be
deceived
         brilliantly
     and without
   pity

and so sometimes it pleases them
       to tell the truth

a few have heard them
singing

and keep it to themselves

red
is
       not
              difficult
everyone
believes
              in
      red

and so the heart

sways a little
              this way
        and that

and is comforted

Magdalena to Her Husband, Balthasar

25 December 1582.

On such a day she writes to him:

The plague, praise God, has again abated with the arrival of
cold weather.

Magdalena, feeling her bones darken, closes the door
against drafts.

She dips her pen, and pauses, sees the raven glide and turn in
sheer extravagant delight.

I too hope, as you write, that God will guide us back together again
in our little garden of joy
and there keep us
together
for a long time.

An opening. A point.
                    ["discover them to be two people in a love-
                        hate relationship"]

She reaches in, one finger at a time. Wider. Her chest hurts
where a little light drifts.

                                    ["with God, their Afflicter
                                        and Redeemer"]

She meant to ask him something, tell him she endures,
and so she writes,

pestilence
            broke out
        in three houses on our street up by the baker's

and three people died

but this was not the thing she meant to say. She needs more light.
The garden! Of course.

And as she settles there, the blossom falls. Petals in her lap.
I am sending you
            with this letter
        the flower

            "[W]e know little   about her   life
                    during the years before her marriage"]

A sign of its virtue: no leaves, no color, no thorns—
but will it last?

                    ["The same may be said for the years
                                    after"]

Bruised, its fragrance chills the air.

It's on its way
        to Balthasar.

Chicory Seeds

1809, a cool dawn. Jefferson looks out
on the blue-eyed fields. Rice-paper light.

The letter flares with its secret.

He thinks of Culpeper: for "sore eyes
that are inflamed"
because its eye-blue flowers sleep at night.

Milk from its stem means
chicory extract
"for nurses' breasts that are pained by the abundance of milk."

(Preposterous, the old Puritan, though robbing
the "proud, insulting, domineering
Doctors,

whose wits were born
five hundred years before themselves," rather pleases him:

the *London Pharmacopoeia* into English for anyone since.
The College of Physicians incensed.)

A sweet hot drink that's not coffee, despite
the Liverpudlian merchants
who ground it up small and made beans.

A livid consumer: "The coffee-dealer adulterates
his coffee with chicory, to increase
his profits,

the chicory-dealer adulterates
his chicory with Venetian-red, to please the eye
of the coffee-dealer;

the Venetian-red dealer grinds up his color
with brick dust,

that by his greater cheapness,
and the variety of shades he offers, he may secure

the patronage of the trade in chicory."

1795: *[A] tolerable sallad for the table*, Jefferson writes
to George W., advised to get some without
delay.

Fourteen years later, President Jefferson "revealed
to be in contact
with the duplicitous British,"

tips his answer
into a cool dry hand:

at last, chicory seeds for George!

He smiles at the confounded patriots
and pockets their pink faces.

At Monticello days gather differently,
eight by eight,

until he is alone in a strange room.

No one has been here before. The walls like cream.
The honey floor.

Pirated from eternity.
Pieces of eight! Pieces of eight!

The seeds in the envelope wait.

Flowers that spread wildly like summer raids,
the ice blue eyes of Viking ghosts
who know this place to be rich.

The clock descends through the floor
and time carries on
its secret work.

Under his feet a new hour blooms.

Tendrils, without roots, like the others.
Duplicitous.

Galen On the Anatomy: Lesson One

Here are the body's principal organs:

    heart
    brain
    liver
    testicles

The heart is a tiny sun drying
the body's amnesia: humidity

causes the soul to forget
what it formerly knew.

So, like a cipher, the pulse ebbs
and flows in its right equation,

secretly telling the days of life.
When we produce by means

of food and drink a good bodily
temperament (*eucrasia*), we thereby

influence the soul towards goodness,
(though do not forget the brain,

for here in the brain rise the nerves
like fountains. They lift and spill

downward from silence. They carry
the soul in its sheath of light.)

Of the liver, Zeno is reported to have said
that he was affected by wine

just as are bitter lupines when soaked
in water. Likewise, when the testicles are heavy

the nerves will stretch like a harpstring
aiming itself at an unseen wound.

But why, when the body is excessively
chilled or overheated, does the soul

definitely leave it? After much search
I have not found out why.

Fig

Elizabeth Blackwell to Alexander Blackwell
September, 1736. The Society of Apothecaries Garden.

My love, though you have driven me to such
intemperate means of living apart
from you, almost in exile, among herbs
and plants of physick, I do bless your poor
habits with such poor praise as best I can
in early morning pilgrimage to cut
new purses, fat and green, among my plants.

My little house in Swan Walk seems to me
the kindest reference to my gosling state
on point of transformation: a lady once
of no ambition, now my secret heart
flares to green fire, my philosopher's stone
alive, new buds and shortly, now, new fruit.

O see how changed I am! that mix of things
seems no more curious than the muddy spring
from which decay we blossom—dear Blackwell,
your dainty girl's a dirty one. This day
one fool said, *milady apothecary*
as I pas't, all in contempt, but I bowed
and smiled sweetly. A fig, if I may say—

and so I chose this afternoon to draw
the charming fig, and find a perfect five-
point leaf spread like a bright concealing hand
across the secret places of our lives,
and, if we've heard the story right, across
the secret places of our first parents;

but lest you think I do descend too far,
remember had she never sinned, Eva
never had been Ave. These things I thought
as I slit open one ripe purple fig,
the wrinkled purse of its velvet skin
filling the palm of my hand, its sticky
seeds so many, packed so close together,
it seemed I held the fruit of paradise,
and felt my woman's spirit rise and eat.

Surinam

Maria Sybilla Merien, artist on a 1699 expedition to Surinam

Dolphins cleave the uncut waters, green as jade from Surinam.
They send me this vision: all roads lead away from Surinam.

Not morning yet, I walk the sea-sprayed deck, a brush
That swells with wet and thunderous grays, too far from Surinam.

Do you think loss is only personal? No doubt it is.
I crouch on English rocks, I gather bitter waves from Surinam.

In the studio, sick and pale, I cut and eat a crust of scarlet
Kept for fever, chills & blindness—in short, in case of Surinam.

Nothing works. My husband's dull, the servants deaf,
And I am mute, because my thoughts are phrased in Surinam.

I copy leaves that burn, entanglements of tendrils, fronds along
The sea-shed sand, creased like a letter. It arrives, erased,
        from Surinam.

Faint wash of sky. You shrug: your coat seems tight. Come close—
No. Closer. Ah, you see? Like that, the palm trees sway in Surinam.

Words fall dead as money. Pocket of grief, stain of joy. On the pure
Page, shrubby scratches. There is no place called Surinam.

So now, Maria, sybil of Christians, choose the colors—saffron, lapis,
Cochineal—which tell (like news heard in a shell) the days
        of Surinam.

When I die, you will see I told the truth. Unfold the skin,
Unwall the heart. You'll find it burning still, the way to Surinam.

Violet Crossing

Collecting seeds in Russia, near the Chinese border

Near the border
feral cliffs swim
in sea fog, pinned
to the edge with

tall fragrant pines.
We crawl through grass
like spies looking
for secret maps.

An outhouse, then—
the only one
in four long miles
of nothing else

but cloud, fog, cliff
where Russia meets
China, and both
suspect the worst,

as we suspect
them both. And as
I close the door
of the outhouse,

I step onto
sweet Russian grass,
starred with Manchur-
ian violets.

Gladiolus

John Tradescant the Younger to Dr. Parkinson
24 July 1642. The Barbary Coast.

Huge
bowl beaten to
shine and froth,
its light
the flaming sword
of eden—azure,
lapis, turquoise,
sapphire, none of
them has told it
right; we lean into
the spray that
stings and scours
our eyes because
the warning is
merciful—it is true
we cannot survive
paradise,
or truthfully, I
think the English
can't, unless you
count the suet
pudding of a sky
and sea we
long for, haven,
miracle enough to
burn the vision
out of me, already
spent with looking:
just this morning

(the coast a glare
behind us now)
some two or three
of us strolled
out of camp to see
the second warning
rise up in a field
of thousands—
stiff green towers
scissoring the
wind, *xiphon*,
corn-flag
fluttering,
glad-sword, sky-
blood, tribe of
spears bearing flowers.

The Ginseng Hunter Finds Jimsonweed

I am considering how to send back to you

days without rage, clouds folded,
rain in jars, still falling,

when the singular bell of jimsonweed calls me

to its fifteen minutes of fame
like a muezzin's promise of joy,

bruised edge of each sprung petal
bleeding inward,

then wider, deeper, a fragrant throat tilts
and the night bends down,

a cricket shirs—everything casts its fate
into the itch of twilight.

"Venus is afflicted," my astrologer told me,
"Your love affairs will be troubled,"

but I say jimsonweed burns,

I say maybe
we have fewer choices than we think,

only a slow and tentative
slip of green

trembling toward the light while night blossoms.

The best I can do is stay away.

Lemon Grass

Poirot sits calmly, expecting disaster, and Miss Lemon
Fetches it for him—letter (from Russia? Imperial seal?),
Though it's barely seven hundred years since Temujin

Rode into his vision (dropping his whip as he yields
to a sea of wildgrass : scimitars swimming in light!
crying *here you must bury me*)—and Europe reeled

Into the new world, its own vision melting to sight
In a yellow wildfire six thousand miles from the heaven
Of prairie. Ah, but the new world spreads like a blight

Microscopically into white pages, crisp and even,
Where Poirot, that clever little dick, is still combing
His Belgian moustaches, curiously tasting of lemon.

Three Wise Men Seek the Emblem of Life in a Jar of Vinegar

(a tale from the Book of Tea)

They found the jar at last, nippling the hill.
Confucious waved and the caravan stopped.

Tents of blue silk. Green hush. They sat still
for eight days, and then he climbed to the top.

Ah, what a ripeness! he dipped in a finger. "Swill!"
he cried, staggering back. "Grief is less sharp!"

He gave way to Sakyamuni. "Friend, I now will
discover the truth." Alas, disappointment! Bitter as hops!

Laotse approached and said with a charming smile:
"Can this be? Such nectar!" and he drank it all up.

And they went away. But around the empty jar on the hill
the wild sage grew up in three colors, a most philosophical crop.

Four Thieves Vinegar

(Four thieves, sentenced to carrying away victims of the plague in Paris, reputedly drank a mixture of vinegar and garlic, and to this attributed their escape from contagion.)

Stench and sting of the fires. Morning a dim of ash. Evening a starless fog.

It is good for ye burning heat of ye head.

"I've stolen nothing," the first thief objected. "Your words or mine, who'd know?"
        He poured a libation over his skull.

"I have a terrible memory," said number two. "I confess to remembering everything."
        He took up the bottle and drank.

Vinegar doth raise an appetite.
And being supped up it casteth out leeches that were drank.

"I have lived without faith for so long," said the third, "I've begun to have doubts."
        He sprinkled a few drops over the flames.

And being gargarized restraineth also ye fluxes in ye throat.

The last thief, who never spoke, said
the usual thing,

And they picked up the dead woman and carried her to the fires.

That the Character of the Soul Depends Upon the Constitution of the Body

*[T]here are three kinds of soul: one is located in the liver,
another in the heart, and another in the brain.*
                                                    Galen

credo
The mouth being small tells you nothing. A secret
holds. Lips cling together

in thin resistance to flesh and air.
Say it's not so.

Didn't you swallow something you shouldn't?

Fat seals, you know
what she paid for *those* lips.

Don't take my word for it. Make up your own.

kyrie
First there is light. You think it is whole
and pure, and you bathe your face in
its unfiltered truth. Then you learn

about clouds, about ions, about the whole
chaos of sky and the way it lied

about who's in charge.

Splinters. Clots.
Division begins its work by subtraction.

That day the sky breaks over you like an ornament

and you hear a voice saying, "The shards
work their way into the heart,

but you won't know the day
or the hour." At this point you even give up
the organic hash.

One late afternoon on your way to the ocean
you look over Hollywood's hills to the shock

of a pale green fissure of sky
small as a catscratch, a slit so fragile

only the delicate bones of birds
can take in its meaning.

Here is one you invent:

You don't have to live
without mercy.

ave
Once Leonardo had marred its
perfection he abandoned

the stone
to that blockhead, Buonarotti,

and went back to flying machines,
goes the legend. Dark center

of bells swung on the thighs
like a shout

only the stone-mason heard.

Down from the shoulder the arm
like a cloak

unfolds
to the tender wrist

and the fingers curled under
in shadow as if

what he hides there
could save us.

Light creeps into its hollow.

Can't you smell it from here? Terror
tangles the air

in its soft gray fist. Let the head
take care

of itself, there's no help
for the rest of him working the hollow again

and again,

where God put his burning finger on Jacob
throwing him out of joint,

to keep him
from running away.

IV

Orange Bang

April's a hat made of rain and an anchor of cloud.

The Santa Monica sea waves goodby and goes back to its sewing.

I bought a small quilt by the pier, it was covered with ants
bearing needles.

Some of us feel this way and some of us that, but mostly
otherwise.

He said, Just who do you think you are, and I said, Exactly.

They sent me a small brown scrap as the proof that my box had
exploded.

Such an agreeable color, like snails sliding over leaves.

I have reassembled my life in another body, one without sin.

In another city, inside a tunnel of wind.

Arrival

The hill dips down, banking its final descent
as we hope for a pleasant stay

here in the Los Angeles region, or wherever
our final destination may be. Lies spent,

teeth cleaned, fingernails swabbed in palmolive,
a dark gray trail of disaster lights my way

back to a difference of lying, one sliver
a day until anything's easy to forgive. A spray

of mistletoe takes on an aura, though never
that sibilant crisp of leaves underfoot.

The old priest cuts the emblem of life
from its vampiric hold on an oak. I'm saying

nothing to love. She still can't sever
sadness from bliss, though she's good with a knife.

In this Direction

*This is a beautiful country. I have not cast my eyes over it before,
that is, in this direction.*
                                    —John Brown, December 2, 1859

Blossom and Meg take the Hollywood Line,
two girls heading west. The American dream's
gone funny somehow—Blossom, in green
fatigues and cowboy boots

has that pinched look around the waist
as if God, feeling peevish, was closing his fist
when it seemed more amusing, a nice twist,
to make Blossom a man

with expensive tastes in nylon and hats.
Across from our bus stop, at Parkman and Sunset,
two cops have arrested a black man who wanted
I remember a double espresso

and make it quick. A middleaged king
in exile, he stands there, maybe thinking
of how long it will be, years of thin
burnt water, refuting

the very idea of *coffee*, while they snap
on the cuffs. Meanwhile Meg is happy
just to be seen with Blossom on a trip,
with the rapt fan's

attentive crossing of legs, the cigarette
flicked with a casual consequence, wet
lips pursed. But she'll never get
that perfectly bored expression

only the rich can acquire,
the ones who have already met desire
and passed through, possibly wiser,
free to take any direction.

Dinner at the Reel Inn

Malibu feels like an old shoe tonight,
leathery, dark, invisibly
smelling of seaweed. Too much sand.
No vacancy at the Topanga Ranch Motel,
but who's staying? You got out
your atlas, and talked about heading east.
We figured the Grand Canyon had to be somewhere
south of Nebraska, but was it in Utah? Arizona?
and then the Badlands, Dinosaur National Monument —

Postcards arrive like news
from a star no longer living.

You thought it took years
to reach the point of departure,
nerves unfolding like sea anemones
dancing to Brahms, but it's only
a phone call, a letter, the hand
on your shoulder, and everything
falls away, bad burritos, the Novel Café,
the shag-headed man in his sandy blanket,

and L.A.'s flatter, brighter,
thinner than ever, its mind
pressed over yours like a re-run
of *Vertigo*, wanting to keep you blonde
and vulnerable, plucking you
out of the harbor, not letting you go,
not letting you leave forever.
But you do.

The blackened nerves of America
wave, beckoning onward, and the day
shifts into reverse.

A Thousand and One Nights

Kay Nielsen , Illustrator (1886-1957)

Return to Copenhagen from Hollywood, California, 1938

Wherever I look, bleakness: somehow it suits me,
the blank sky, the scrawled water, rubbed hills.
When the snows arrive I remember the hills
in Hollywood, glutted with tired flowers, the sea

breaking and breaking, its wet foamed frills
like the abandoned gown of Scheherazade, trying
to get back to her. What for? We both can rely
on illusion, but only in darkness or snow will the spells

finish their dangerous beauties—against sky
are the clouds set forever, unmaking their perfect
faces, their jeweled thighs, formed and wrecked
by the same mouth. Slender and unafraid I

made her, the curve of her back a crescent,
the curve of her hand outstretched in the story's
vision, her ornamental king slumped in mysterious
yielding before her pale body. What I meant,

what I wanted to say there by the sign of her knees
bare and commanding I no longer remember.
Something to do though with power and trembling,
with love and its endings, with brave-told lies.

Is

(on The Fall of Troy, Romare Bearden, 1974)

for two voices

i.
halves and crosses,
night-smoke,
totem-faced building
white metal horse and
green fishes
helen a burntout
lap becomes a pier-
brown robe: three
sing (*laudant, laudamus*) to
siva who rises
phoenix: life out of ash

ii.
two sides of any story:
green morning
shakes red dreadlocks, a brilliant
cerulean eye that sees
above lapis lazuli water
shade whose
cross unfolding
black warriors they
praise him,
life out of ashes
(*est*): sing, for he

Is.

Camellias for P

(named for Georg Josef Kamel, Moravian Jesuit missionary, 1706)

Camellias, unexpected, garish
as the bright pink kneesocks
Mrs. Eichelberger wears
on Sundays when she walks

to church, despite the best advice
of neighbors (not quite friends)
seem undecipherable, the petals
frilled and heavy, dense

with color. Everything expands
except camellias. And yet
the scent—a fresh and rainy smell,
so light, so delicate.

Bent above his graftings, Father
Kamel checks for buds,
for signs of chaos channeled into life.
Patience. Water. Mud.

The tree releases blooms the way
old ladies lose their gloves,
address books, everything except
the memory of old loves.

Some five or six are floating in a bowl
of water. When he knew
that he'd invented these peculiar
Slavic, brilliant jewels,

he picked the lot and scattered them
about the feet of Christ
(but named them for himself). Old love,
will you and I survive

the yellow cat who won't come in
but cries at 3 a.m.
for someone who will not come out?
Below, a window slams

resentfully. The one good eye of darkness
blurs, enlarges, focuses
his outline on the stairs, the whiskers
twitching as he pokes

the slit of warm air underneath
the door. Since I know what's not
fastened tends to drift, I hold
my head. Another shot

of Robitussin. Back to bed.
You're in your second sleep
by now, will fling an arm across
my pillow, drifting deep

as the snow I think of sometimes
covering camellias.

A Norman Milkmaid at Greville

(*Jean-Francois Millet, 1871*)

i.
Nothing much to see, a girl staggering
down a footpath in 1871. Greville
is far behind her now, the dairy
one small slash of white
floating in a far green sea.

What's all that to the distance
between us? I can't imagine
her desires beneath the dark warmth of cattle,
scarfed head pressed into all that dusty hide
with the rhythm of the downpull
and the steam rising from the still-cold buckets.

Now she leans before me: hip thrust out
to balance that awkward shuffle,
two thongs looped around her arm
and drifting hand, basket on her shoulder
full of milk smoking in the chill.
How many layers, three? Four?
wrapped around her feet—
or are those wooden shoes?

Dark dark the receding light—
blooming or tightening, I can't tell which.

ii.
What's missing then, what seems
beyond us? Grief? Nothing so intense.
Only gray-flocked canvas, chunks of blue,
a weary resignation, walking dreams . . .
the edge of moor there. *That* seems immense.

iii.
Thirty first-graders crowd the room,
silent as sparrows stunned by a wall of glass.

The teacher gestures toward a painting
filled with garnet and emerald green,
a pheasant cock hanging by a bowl of grapes

and golden candelabras, red cabbage
exposing its heart in frilled edges,
the very splinters in a wooden crate
of ripe tomatoes—ecstatic—!

Do you see anything moving
in this painting? asks the teacher.

A small girl raises her hand.
The peach is rolling across the table.

No, no, smiles the teacher, a little tightly.
This is what we call a Still Life.
The twenty-nine children nudge each other,
grinning, and the group moves on.

She stands there, watching the peach roll,
so brilliant in light it burns the cheeks.

iv.
—all of her body in shadow
eyes closing, mouth askew

as if a Mardi Gras had passed her on the road
and left her still asleep.

Light is approaching, but she faces
into darkness, she is struggling
towards us.

v.
Across the room old Satan marks
her progress. Minutes bronze
and gather in his wings. But she bores him,
they all bore him, no vision anymore,
no grand ambition!
He'd welcome
any kind of challenge—
except aesthetic, which bores him also.

And now the rage is all for dissolution.

Boring.

A glance at the girl again, the bruises
meant for eyes. A stifled sigh.
Oh yes the way
is difficult, torturous even,
but she'll arrive.

79

vi.
A sharp smell pricks the air,
a shudder of instinct—not felt that
for years! He can't move his head,
neck stiff with centuries of boredom,
but the gaze of him flames out—
a young child stares into that inward flaring socket,
mutely, mildly curious, eating a peach.

Vampire Movies

He was Panama black, "like a hat," he said, saving
his Spanish for later. He did wear his life
at an angle.

                I am he tells me the white
goddess he's always wanted.
Perfect. Even the shape of betrayal

looks good from this distance
and my throat tilts like a spilled drink.

We rent *Nosferatu* because it reminds him of home.
"He's the proof that everything rises."

I count the moments.

Black scowl and a little hat.
Big teeth.
                Dear terror
I think I'm in love with you.

        (the cats, also—

                they twist their fur in one another's cries
at the swerve of his smile)

No, I'm wrong: that was Mina
fastened to Dracula's breast like an infant.

(curtains would sleep   *between us*   *like windows held still*
   in the hush of snow.   *we were always*
                              astonished by so much sky

which could part cities and not be used up)

Kiss my ear the way Mary caught God
as he tenderly parted the waves of her hair like water

flooding her bones with joy

and I am beside myself.
O rose, I am sick.

There goes the count, hugging his little coffin
since beds are so unreliable.

His legs scissor past. I feel kindly towards him.
I hope he gets something to eat.

Meanwhile redemption sweeps through our lives
like a plague

though I cherish a reasonable doubt. Think of who lingers,

who hangs back, who waits. What twists in the eye's designs.
Who answers the phone still wet and keeps talking.

Who turns off its ring.

It is more dangerous than you think,
whispers Dracula. He takes the razor away for a quick snack.

(music   crackles   like new life
      in his fingertips

                    sheering

        the map of nerves from my skin

which he doesn't need   he knows
        where he's going)

How can I hate him? Love's ruthless as death in its delicate timing:
the brush of his hand
      across years as I open the door,
                      the strange
independence of shadows.

Like stopping for supper, we don't ask why
but when.

Día de los Muertos

Unsafe, this stagger of morning.

I pause at the door
like a thick loaf raisined with sleep

on the cusp of disquiet, the dead oven's
lip of doom—

or the lisp? all hard edges dissolving in mist,
the cup disappearing in steam,

the flat man
stuttering up the driveway with three bags
belching cans,

fixed shine in the eyes that flicker over
me turning the key in my door,
        flicker and slide,

my outline slick as a postcard of Kobe, Japan,
and about as expected,

while the fog spirits us each away.

Yellow cellophane leaves. White paste of sky.

A cold pale light
ghosting everywhere, charmed

by our pulsing bodies that tremble in stillness,
stumble and wheeze,

as we go out to meet it.

Getting Away In South Kerry

On the road to Tralee we pass hedges cunningly planted
to look like L.A. Store fronts wink
and go out.

The same faces fold up like wallets.

In the evening gold shadows leaf through his hair
though he feels no wind.

It's a trick I have.

I follow him in from the dingle where shale spits foam
in a storm of light all the tourists think
is a dangling key.

Then we see the bruise dimpling across the water.

We gasp as the sky rolls up and I can't find
the camera. Over the tidal basin stars hatch
and fly up like cinders.

Everyone said, Nothing's as good as finally getting away.

What rosy curls! He talks about fish and his friends
in Laguna. It's been so long, he'd like to see them,
but where would he stay?

Dark pours into my glass in a slow wave of panic.
The moon ignites.

My ribs open like fingers and wait for what happens.

His voice swims in the mirror dissolving
around my fist.

I can feel my hips sparkling as they tune up and then my body
shrinks to a mouth.

I think I shall sing.

At last, I think, life! Now
I'm getting somewhere.

V

Lycos Search: [Adoptions: Not found. Replace with?]

[?adopt]

L. se alicui adoptare (Obs.)
We are made sons of God by adoption
As Chickens are hatcht at Grand Cairo by the Adoption
of an Oven.

Thus we have adopted the modern German names
of several rocks and minerals, as *gneiss*, *hornblende*,
quartz, and *nickel*.

The Spirit itself, that is the Spirit of Adoption,
which Christians receive,
is one Witness
I had rather adopt a child than get it.

To approve, to confirm, then,

I propose that the report and accounts be adopted
which [words] must depend for their adoption
on the suffrage of futurity:
L. fac ramam ramus adoptet, as Ovid says, (Obs.)
or as Holland when he read Pliny in 1601,

"Fit one [vine stocke] to the other, ioyning pith
to pith, and then binding them fast together so close that no
aire may enter
between, vntill such time as the one hath adopted
the other."

[?adorn with pictures]

Now according to the 1959 reprint of a 1934 translation of
De Materia Medica which presents a Greek work of the first
century as understood in Hampshire in the [1500's] illustrated
by a Byzantine artist in AD 512 for presentation to the daughter
of Anicius Olybrius who was Emperor of the West in 472
(the drawings learned from "originals . . . not far removed
from sketches by the famous Crateus, whose plant-descriptions
are occasionally quoted in the text")

we are less likely to invent than to mistake,

[?adore]
    and so I bless

the Nestorians, who first believed, in error, that the son
of God was only by Adoption,

    and I bless

the pictures, which as Pliny warns,
are deceitfull; in representing such a number of colours,
and especially representing the lively
hew of Hearbs according to their nature as they grow,

no marvell if they that limned and drew them out, did fail
and degenerat from the first pattern and
originall, and as in error they misunderstood
the wanderings of each plant
from its picture, *for they change*
and alter their form and
shape every quarter of the year, depending on the place in which
the root
of their deviance may be found,

[?adulterate]

   and I bless

the figures which seem hopeless of interpretation,
for they are printed in the hope that
field-botanists when traveling in the special localities whence
the Dioscoridean flora was derived, may thus recognize
a few of the plants which through mistaken
features it has been impossible to identify in an herbarium
of dried plants,

for so these imperfect identifications stimulate by their falsity
the production of a revised version

   and I bless

the Gnostics, also Adoptionists who formed, in error,
the division of the cosmos into spiraled chambers reached
by strange enchanted turnings between light
and darkness, stairs that wind
the spirit up its thread

   and I bless

the woman who believed herself incapable of love
and so chose for herself the sergeant whose red hair burnt her
husband to a crisp
when she mistook him as my father
(for I have no father, and have never had)

   and thus I bless

the air which fills my body in its rising
and descent,
and I adore the strange digressions of my life
adorned with pictures
from the error of her ways.

Speech in Five Acts

on meeting a birthmother

Mariposa, California.

[genitive]

expensive elsewhere, your hunger kisses its bowl of ink, you would do anything, anything so i'd lie down in this brown clench of hills and forget i was going or thinking of someplace unherded or held. why bother? poor i was born, a chipped plate and a fork full of dents, i am here now, subside, desist, i lie down and i claim my inheritance, blade by blade.

[subjunctive]

coolie in blue jeans, coolie in sweet grass yellow in august, coolie rocks. if a coolie in blue jeans were willing to wear a hat made of sweet grass, the hungry, riddled yellow, itching and harrowed, the fitful grass in august to get to the other side. of these rocks

[dative]

what do you bring the lilies? there is to be sparing of the lilies. to the lilies it will be pleasing. from this we augur days and fallows, the anhinga ruptures the lake, though the wound is made small, almost invisible. it seeps there, in water, among the lilies. would you please send me your catalog of lilies.

[relative]

weed me, o night, i am wracked with green. i spit like a cricket, i
rise in a whir of wings thinner than candlelight shining through
fingers—grasshoppers, my cousins, embrace your lost defect, do
not despise what you know, my familiars are strange to me now,
and why should you not be familiar? though they waver, their
edges corrupt with joy, white stones scattered like stars in a lunar
panic of grass.

[imperative]

blue shards brilliant and sharp as a child who owns nothing, and vast it is. lunatic fringe of sky, what have you to say? too much and too little, the back of a dress too small on a fat man, trees tightened up into knots on the puckered fields. let's hurry boys. aren't the boys hurrying? let us not stay at home. he is one who. when we have gone down into italy, the romans will not be able to resist us. there is no one who. there is nothing that. the snow is so deep i can scarcely walk. do not trust the gauls. they will certainly betray you. let us not stay at home. when the parrot had died, corinna was very sad. o nine times terrible, bless me, my mothers, for i am singed.

Hymn for a Birthmother

I.

She is the voice in the wilderness crying.

She is not prepared.

She is the shadow of legs crossing the light like a fan.

She is the ultraviolet message to bees.

She is on her way.

She is the neon hinge of night.

She is the window closing.

She is the lawnchair's last warm curve.

She is the one who looked back.

She is the mouth forming *o*.

She is the panic of waves.

II.

I am the tongue that will lick her clean.

I am the wound that will not grieve.

I am the broken needle in her arm.

I am the light that travels too slowly to see.

I am the hiss in the sand.

I am the red stone considering fire.

I am the circle she walks inside.

I am the crow that walks there with her.

I am the sidewalk telling news.

I am the crooked sign on the last hotel that says *no*.

I am the one that got away.

Hole

Her hands raw in the wound-up days sprung loose,
that baffled whir of time she ignores
easy as a once-aching tooth dangling on a
thread (*gawd, Myrtle,* and she'd just smile, digging out onions,
another hole never hurt nobody)
which might explain how a place so flat and basically holeless
could get to be called a hole,
as in no-water-hole,
dust-hole,
black hole of whatever,
the whole enchilada of holes,
and so it was a kind of mission to make a few more holes
for the relief of other folk trapped in this two-dimensional
pitiless cartoon of a hole
nothing but gophers and onions could ever get out of,
not even the daughter who stands there like a worn-down penny
in the last rub of light, saying *i gotta get outa here,*
i want my own life, saying, *i wanta be somethin,*
so she don't even look up
at the bite of that hole going in because no matter what
she knows she won't be left here for long all alone
with six babies and two half-grown,
because sometimes what seems like an empty hole
turns out to have plenty going for it after all
and anyway, she thinks, turning the black dirt over
and punching a place for the seed,
that's the way of holes, sometimes you stand there for a long
time at the edge
before dropping a stone to see how far—
but the girl ain't that kind, she won't fall through,
she's the kind so afraid of the hole she'll carry it everywhere,
shooting up in her chest like an onion, pungent and thin
till they smell her coming and know she's a child of the hole,
until dread finally rivets her gaze and she learns to dig.

Gingkos

November undoes Division Street—
a derangement of trees

like so many broken music stands

freed to an improvised
scat of days,

each maple's last spray of red
a trash of wet noise.

Zero weather
closes in.

Night pocked with predictable stars,

familiar feint of rain,
all the same dead words underfoot,

the tiring maples blink their red alerts in the margin,
"Details! Explain! Develop!"

but no one listens. How can we, cast
in the passive voice of winter?

And then without warning a scribble of sky bends
childishly close,

the maples twirl their last rags of confetti

and all down the street
gingkos rattle their still-green leaves

like old money
thrown in a fit of joy to the poor.

Time Piece

I know what time is, but if someone asks me, I cannot tell him.
— St. Augustine

[relativity]

The genes tell nothing of all this sparkle, the mist and forgotten teeth and the trinkets of blood. They give nothing away. They are into preserving. You might think a judgment belongs. You might think an airy dismissal. One of the stories my genes unzip: you are not wrong to love a fraud. So long as you do not kiss him. Then it is oola la trouble in paradise, out of your garden and into the jungle. But the fraudspawn is something else, button of jelly topping the foam. It will find you when least. You expect it. And then the unravelling. Does not connect to new twisting, the wrist in its packet of bruise, the chest with its telltale crack, the rerouted flow. Not. Yet

[escapement]

Out to the movies, a dinner for two, we touch but we do not join. We roll up together, finite but no boundaries or edges, so how can we touch? Slide and glissando. Fingernails bleeding. Tip of the finger to all that. It's just you and me baby so don't you forget it, I know where you live. Inside me she keeps expanding but finds no leak and no finish, she does not remember this meadow, though something about the crepuscular slither of ocean reminds her of something she knew once, when all that she knew was nothing. Escapement, that brief interruption, the tick. And release. Of a watch. Going. Around. And around. Interruption advances the truth.

[water clock]

Weight of "I know" follows "I think" in a fluid circle, dip and rise of the soul. Sometimes a balloon, giddy and red, and then two, they expand and deflate together. Each side has something to offer, heart, kidney, ovary, track of the belly. Ins and outs. Is everything locked and shut off? Beware of the enemy you don't know means including you. Now I uncurl from looking. I am unfolding my fists. Dear enemy, face I own, father I never will, militant rage I exact your obedience. Wash me and I shall be. Neither will I fear. When courage falls, the night will get up. It will strike, and the nerves will hear it. Pain has a beautiful sound. Exquisite.

[transitive]

Einstein snagging himself again on the same damn nail which will not be hammered or pulled. It is absurd. It is not a reasonable nail. It hangs there, in nothing, serene. He knows about time. He knows about space. He is not sure nothing can be known for certain. "Contradictory," he writes Bohr, "to every idea of reality that is reasonable," so probably true and contagious. Those of us who escape always think there's a reason. Those of us who do not know there is. Shrapnel and zinfandel, we drink to the town we were almost in and the child gives up his blasted eye. Leap of fate, act of will. He thinks of it rolling in heaven, watching the places he's never been. O now he will see, he will know in time. Where are we going. We have always been here.

Tea

(Japanese Tea Room, University of Michigan Art Museum)

a stone turns into a step
at the child-high door

it is like my life
opaque and miraculous

poised at a rabbit hole

door i must bow myself
door i must creep

the scroll on the wall explains everything
differently each time

o riches of here and be

not is a tight word
nothing undoes it

impossible little room
you are open

without fear of business

i lean on your missing walls each day
i lean on your slit of light

i see into the nothing you hold exact
and precarious

on the tokonoma
three sprays of orchid

a petal clings

like the last good man

like the slipshod grace of backbone
curved in a hiss

unable to speak or unclench

door i am not permitted to enter
until i am light as a shadow

although my head is an echo
my heart is a pocket

my pocket a tunnel of sighs

i am a pitcher
without water

cup without tea

o little room let me in
i have already

lost the way

The Ginseng Hunter Lies Down In a Meadow

I love the sky which is not the color of grief.
If there is an argument, it is an old argument

sky carries on with itself and has nothing to do with us.
It says nothing of the life I was going to live, back then,

before I understood there is no future, only
a kind of forward wash carried out of the last act

I thought could be changed in time to prevent its arrival.
When sky is this confused we call it rain

and go in for the day. Among its stars not one
fails for lack of vision, its light rubbed thin

on a cinderblock, only another long narrow box
for keeping us out of each other's lives

as if all it took were walls. Stars fall out
of their places because it is time to go but nobody

locks the door behind them or sends on the mail.
Sky rearranges no mirrors and tells no lies

about what it was thinking when you met
its gaze for the last time over coffee

and foam which obscured the muted underlight
of the throat swallowing. The sparrow has no more space

than the hawk to dive and roll and sky touches
neither but hovers there distant and still imperceptibly

present, though if you have enough little bits of sky
heaped together it glows or streaks or ignites

without purpose. Sky can be wounded
but does not heal like the skin we mistake it for.

There is a language of moisture and heat but when sky
makes a point it does not invite dialogue.

I love the sky which takes no prisoners. It kills
like an elephant no longer able to restrain its itch

and so whole jungles and villages are trampled in something
that looks like rage but is only relief, for sky

does not roll itself up or reveal a long sweet curve
of leg emerging from water, neither stretching nor leaning

nor any other thing the leg may do, and so
we search sky daily for signs of our lost selves as if

so much indifference must surely hide something, and where
else could all that feeling have gone? But sky isn't even

indifferent. It tells us no more than the wind, which is not
the sound of something tearing a long way off,

or a cough, or a sigh of bewilderment. The sky I love
is the sky that is not suffused with faith or delusion

or joy or poignant arousal shaped like a new
understanding of sadness, and this is the sky I look for

now without ceasing, the way ivy creeps
toward the light, but to tell you the truth I have yet to see it.

Notes

Weathering St. Cloud: For Jim Lundin. St. Cloud is a small town south of Kissimmee, Florida, where a bizarre rash of tornados struck during the 1998 El Niño.

In the Roof Garden: For Elisabeth Frost and Derek Hackett on their wedding (March, 1998).

Herbal Remedies: For Bevan.

Magdalena to Her Husband, Balthasar: Based on Steven Ozment's 1986 edition of letters exchanged between a sixteenth-century Nuremberg merchant and his wife. The bracketed quotations are from Ozment's introduction.

Chicory Seeds: Nicholas Culpeper (1616-54) was a Puritan apothecary whose pithy vehemence makes his Herbal well worth reading in its original version, partly because of his absolute belief in the Doctrine of Signatures, which held that God had left clues in the characteristics of any plant as to its use—heart-shaped plants were sure cardiac cures, and so on. Culpeper produced his English translation of the official London Pharmocopoeia (with much commentary) as a deliberate attempt to provide common people with medical knowledge and agency, to the displeasure of the Royal College of Physicians. Jefferson's passion for all things botanical pressed him to continue correspondence with "the duplicitous British," including the incident mentioned. The livid consumer is cited from Rodale's *Encyclopedia of Herbs* (1986 edition).

Fig: Elizabeth Blackwell (d. 1758) was perhaps the first woman apothecary; her *Curious Herbal* was published in weekly parts and collected in two large volumes in 1737 and 1739. She drew, engraved, and painted all 500 plates herself. Apparently she did this in order to release her husband from debt— unfortunately, Alexander Blackwell went to Sweden without his wife and was subsequently tried and executed for the high treason of plotting to change the royal succession. She lived near the Chelsea Society of Apothecaries Garden in a street called "Swan Walk" while working on the herbal.

Galen on the Anatomy: Galen was Marcus Aurelius' private physician; his teachings and prescriptions formed the basis of European medicine until Paracelsus' introduction of mercury and antimony in the therapeutic, rather than humoral (the four humors of hot, dry, cold, wet) system of medicine. Early physicians disagreed about the primary organs and their functions. It was actually Plato who said that the body's moisture caused the soul to become forgetful of what it once knew. Galen, though he was careful not to refute Plato, was troubled by his own inability to locate and define the soul.

Gladiolus: Dr. John Parkinson (1567-1650) was perhaps the most famous herbalist of his day, apothecary to both James VI and Charles I. He is best known for two works: *Paradisus Terrestris* (1629), primarily a florilegium (an herbal about flowers) and *Theatrum Botanicum* (1640), the most comprehensive book of medicinal plants in English at the time. Parkinson said that "John Tradescant assured me, that hee saw many acres of ground in Barbary spread over with [gladioli]" (*Paradisus Terrestris*).

The Ginseng Hunter Finds Jimsonweed: Jimsonweed blooms open quickly enough to watch and last for one night only, beginning at dusk; the flower wilts by mid-morning of the next day. Jimsonweed is a notorious hallucinogen, one highly unreliable in potency and so one of the most unpredictable narcotic herbs.

Violet Crossing: For David Michener, botanist and Curator of the Matthai Botanical Gardens, University of Michigan (Ann Arbor), who told me this story.

Lemon Grass: Temujin: Genghis Khan.

Four Thieves Vinegar: The quotations are from Dioscorides' *De Materia Medica*.

Dinner at the Reel Inn: For Katherine Swiggart.

Camellias for P: For Karl, who knew Putney and Tango.

Lycos Search: "Lycos search" is one of the search engines on the World Wide Web. The queries are from the list called up with Microsoft Word 5.1's spelling dictionary. Other sources include the *Oxford English Dictionary* ("adopt" and "adoption"), Pliny's *Natural History*, and the preface to the 1959 reprint of the 1934 edition (using the original John Goodyer translation) of Dioscorides' *De Materia Medica*, probably the best-known herbal surviving from classical times.

Speech in Five Acts and Hymn for a Birthmother: On meeting my birthmother for the first time in August, 1997.

Hole: For my maternal biological grandmother, Myrtle Arlene.

Gingkos: For my students.

Tea: Tokonoma : the altar in a tea house. For the poet R. Tillinghast.

photo by Bill Wood

A native of Florida, Deanne Lundin has lived in Oklahoma, Boston, Los Angeles, and Ann Arbor. Lundin's poems have appeared in *The Georgia Review, Prairie Schooner, The Kenyon Review, Colorado Review, Antioch Review* and elsewhere. She has earned degrees from the Eastman School of Music and the University of Michigan, where she now teaches. Current writing projects include her dissertation (English, UCLA) on American women poets and their use of mystical discourse; and a memoir based on the experience of being adopted and her recent reunion with her birth family.